D1243405

Ancient City A to Z

A St. Augustine Alphabet Book

To Avery & Olivia
From Grandma Mary
& Grandpa Andy!
April. 2017

By Rob Hicks

Illustrated by Cynthia Pierson

Island Media Publishing, LLC
120 N. 15th St.
Fernandina Beach, FL 32034
www.islandmediapublishing.com
Printed in China

ISBN 978-0-9829908-1-0
Library of Congress 2013918991

Island Media Publishing, LLC

A is for Ancient City,
St. Augustine, historic and pretty.
It is here that the Spanish landed centuries ago
and from where this history continues to grow.

The area that is now St. Augustine was first visited by Europeans in the early 1500s. In 1565 Pedro Menendez arrived and established a mission. He named the area St. Augustine because he first sighted land on August 28th which was the feast day of Augustine of Hippo, an important leader in the Christian faith. The first Catholic Mass held in the New World took place in St. Augustine as well as the birth of the New World's first European child. Menendez quarreled with the French Huguenots who had settled just to the north in the area near what is now Jacksonville. He eventually executed a large number of the Huguenots.

St. Augustine is the oldest continuously occupied European establishment in the United States. Today, the "Ancient City" is considered the area of St. Augustine where the Spanish had their earliest establishments. St. Augustine has grown out of this area into a town that has played an important role throughout Florida's history. Over the years, it has evolved into a popular tourist destination, but it has been able to keep the memory of its Spanish beginnings alive.

B is for the Bridge of Lions that spans the bay
joining the mainland and island along Highway A1A.
The four towers mark the style and the lions do too.
It even has a drawbridge so tall boats can pass through.

St. Augustine's Bridge of Lions has been called the most beautiful bridge in Dixie. As part of Highway A1A, it crosses the Mantanzas Bay and connects the Ancient City with Anastasia Island. It was originally built in 1927 by Davis Shores in order to reach the new homes he was building on Anastasia Island. The bridge, complete with its four towers, was designed with a Mediterranean style. It takes its name from the two marble lion statues that guard its entrance. They were modeled after similar lion statues in Florence, Italy, which is also home to many buildings done in the Mediterranean style.

The Bridge of Lions also contains a drawbridge. That means the center of the bridge can lift up to allow boats to pass through. Without this, the Mantanzas Bay, part of the intercoastal waterway, would be impassable by taller boats. The bridge has recently been renovated.

C is for the Castillo de San Marcos, the old Spanish fort
that guarded town and harbor from enemies of all sorts.
The fort is made of coquina, a mix of coral and shell
that withstood attacks from bullets and cannonballs as well.

The Spanish began construction on what would become the Castillo de San Marcos in 1672. Many modifications have occurred to the fort since then. It has served as the main defense for the city for most of its history. When the British attacked Spanish-controlled St. Augustine in 1702, the local citizens all gathered inside the Castillo for shelter. During the Civil War, it was used mainly as a prison for Native Americans and deserters. The National Park Service took control of it in 1933.

The fort is made of a material called coquina. Coquina is a rocky substance found along the coast of Florida that formed as tiny shells bonded together over thousands of years. It is softer than a lot of rocks but still suitable for building. This softness has actually made the fort a safer place. For example, when the British attacked the city in 1702, the fort's wall simply absorbed the cannonballs and bullets shot at it. If the coquina had not been so soft, those same cannonballs could have eventually knocked down the fort's walls.

D is for the dolphins, bottled-nosed and gray
living at Marineland where they jump, flip, and play.
Dolphin encounters are now what the Marineland park features
where you get to pet, feed, and swim with these majestic sea creatures.

Marineland began in 1938 as a movie studio used for underwater footage in films like *Creature from the Black Lagoon*. Many tourists soon flocked to the area to see the collection of sea creatures including the dolphins. By the late 1960s, Marineland was among the top tourist destinations in Florida as people came to see the marine mammals perform acrobatic tricks. In 2006, the park was completely renovated and more changes were made in 2011. The park mostly features dolphin encounters now where guests are able to interact with the dolphins in the water.

The dolphins can also be found swimming wild in the waters that surround St. Augustine. They are mammals, not fish, and actually breathe air. So, they can be spotted from the beach or in the Mantanzas River as they surface to breathe. They usually move in small groups called pods. They work together in these pods to hunt for the fish they eat. The dolphins are able to emit clicking noises and use echolocation to find their prey.

E is for East Florida, a division that pre-dates
Florida becoming a territory and part of the United States.
St. Augustine was the capital on the eastern side.
With Pensacola in the west, Tallahassee soon split the divide.

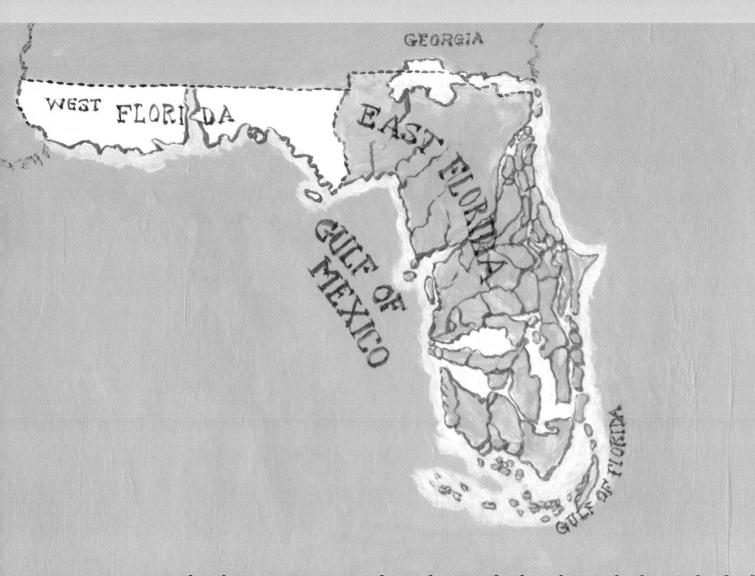

In 1763, Spain lost the Seven Years War and agreed to give Florida to the British. The British split Florida into two sides. Pensacola became the capital of West Florida, and St. Augustine was made the capital of East Florida. In 1783, Florida was returned to the Spanish who decided to keep the division.

In 1819, Spain was forced to turn control of Florida over to the United States. The United States also decided to keep the division between East and West Florida, but it was soon decided that a more central location was needed as the capital. As the story goes, two men set out on horse back—one from St. Augustine and one from Pensacola. The two met in Tallahassee, and so it was decided that it should be the new, more central capital. Florida finally became a state in 1845.

F is for Fort Mose and a community of freed slaves
who came to Spanish Florida for the freedom that they craved.
The fort was made of logs and mud, and the freed slaves lived inside.
From here they guarded St. Augustine when British attacks were tried.

Fort Mose was established by the Spanish in 1738. Its original inhabitants were escaped slaves from the Carolinas. The Spanish in St. Augustine agreed to grant these slaves freedom if they joined the Spanish army and became Catholic. The walls of the fort were made out of logs and mud. Between those walls were little huts where the freed slaves lived. They spent their time farming the land that surrounded Fort Mose.

Lying just north of the Ancient City, Fort Mose served as the first line of defense for St. Augustine. In 1740, the British, led by James Oglethorpe, attacked. Fort Mose was abandoned and destroyed, but a new Fort Mose was constructed by 1752. From this new fort, the freed slaves continued to defend St. Augustine in small skirmishes with the British. Today, the area that once held the Fort Mose community is a state park.

G is for the ghosts that call St. Augustine home.
Some say these old spirits still like to roam
around many old places throughout the ancient town.
So keep your eyes peeled, you may be on haunted ground.

With such a long and rich history, it's no surprise that many people say they have seen ghosts around St. Augustine. The St. Francis Inn, Casablanca Inn, Casa de Solana, Bayfront Marin House, Casa de la Paz, City Gate, Castillo de San Marcos, and lighthouse are all said to be haunted. The lighthouse, for example, is said to be haunted by the ghosts of the lighthouse builder's drowned daughters and a man who fell to his death while painting it. A woman with a lantern is reported to haunt the Casablanca Inn. Guests of the Casa de la Paz claim they've seen the ghost of a woman carrying a suitcase, and the City Gate is said to be haunted by a young girl who died during a yellow fever epidemic. The police have received calls from motorists that claim there is a girl in a white dress standing near the gate and waving at cars.

H is for Henry Flagler, a wealthy oil man
who came from New York to Florida and bought up lots of land.
Then Flagler built a railroad--and hotels, grand and tall.
The Ponce de Leon in St. Augustine might have been the grandest of them all.

Henry Flagler was born in 1830. He worked for a while as a salesman in Ohio before he met John Rockefeller. Flagler and Rockefeller began an oil refinery business called Standard Oil that would soon become the largest oil refinery in the world. As a result, Flagler grew very rich.

Standard Oil was based in New York City, but Flagler came to Florida in 1876 when a doctor told him the weather would be better there for his sick wife. Once in Florida, he visited St. Augustine but noticed it lacked the fine hotels and transportation system needed to attract out-of-state tourists. So, Flagler improved the existing railroads and built the Ponce de Leon Hotel that is now Flagler College. He also built the Alcazar Hotel in St. Augustine. Flagler continued building hotels in Florida and eventually established the city of Miami as a tourist destination.

I is for the island of Anastasia, surrounded on each side
by water that flows in and out according to the tide.
The island is a barrier for the mainland and the marsh
protecting them from winds and waves that can be extremely harsh.

Anastasia Island is a barrier island that sits just off the Florida mainland. It is completely surrounded by water. The east side of the island meets the Atlantic Ocean and the west side meets the Mantanzas River. The island was probably formed about 18,000 years ago as glaciers from an ice age melted and flooded areas behind beach ridges. Sediment deposited by the ocean and rivers carrying material from the mainland also helped construct the island.

A barrier island's main function is to protect the mainland from powerful waves and winds caused by hurricanes and other strong storms. It also provides a habitat for the many animals and insects that live around the island. Many of these animals depend on the tides that rise and fall from the gravitational pull of the sun and moon.

J is for the jaws of alligators and crocodiles
at the St. Augustine Alligator Farm, a haven for reptiles.
The farm's collection of reptiles is, without a doubt, first-rate.
It's also one of the oldest attractions still running in the state.

In 1893, two men opened a souvenir store with a pen of about 40 alligators at the end of a railroad on Anastasia Island. They hoped that tourists coming to see the alligators would buy their souvenirs. The people were more interested in the alligators, however. Their popularity grew and the alligators were moved to their present location in the 1920s. Over time, other animals, including crocodiles, were added to the collection and the farm remains open over 100 years after it began.

The St. Augustine Alligator Farm now teams with researchers from places like the University of Florida to study the unique habits of a variety of reptiles—but most importantly the American alligators. These animals are found all over the southeastern United States, including the waters surrounding St. Augustine. They can grow to be almost 15 feet long and weigh over 1000 pounds.

K is for Dr. King who fought for civil rights, and was arrested in St. Augustine for entering a restaurant that only served whites. Martin Luther's trip to St. Augustine brought segregation to the national newscast, and played an important role in the Civil Rights Act finally being passed.

In the summer of 1964, the civil rights movement was at its height. This movement sought to gain equal rights for African Americans who were not allowed to eat at the same restaurants, use the same bathrooms, or even visit the same beaches as whites. During this time Dr. Martin Luther King Jr. visited St. Augustine. He was arrested when he tried to eat at the Monson Motor Lodge, a hotel, where only white people were allowed. Many of the town's black residents decided to jump in the pool of the hotel and refused to leave in protest. The manager of the hotel poured acid in the pool in order to get the protesters to leave. Pictures of the manager pouring acid into the pool were broadcast on the news all over the country. People in other parts of the United States were outraged and these events in St. Augustine helped lead Congress to finally pass the Civil Rights Act later that summer, giving African Americans equal rights.

L is for the lighthouse, painted black and white,
serving as a beacon for sailors with its revolving light.
Beside the tower sits a home where the lighthouse keeper slept.
For surely he needed lots of rest to climb all 219 steps!

Lighthouses are used by sailors to navigate and to mark the land from the ocean so ships do not run aground. Lighthouses can also be used as watch towers by those on land looking for potential attackers from sea. The location of the St. Augustine lighthouse has served that purpose for a long time.

A wooden watch tower was built at the present location of the lighthouse on Anastasia Island back in the 1500s. A coquina tower was built at the same site by the early 1740s. That was replaced in 1824 and the present tower was built in the 1870s. That lighthouse is now painted with spiraling black and white stripes and there are 219 steps from base to top. The revolving light inside the tower can be seen up to 24 miles away. Before the lighthouse became electric, it burned fuel that needed to be refilled. This was done by the lighthouse keeper who lived in a small house that is still located next to the tower.

M is for Mantanzas, the Spanish word for slaughter.
It's the name on a local fort and St. Augustine bodies of water.
The fort was built at the inlet to guard St. Augustine from attack,
and the river's marshy waters create an important habitat.

St. Augustine has a fort, river, and inlet all sharing the name Mantanzas. The name came to the area after Pedro Menendez and his Spanish troops slaughtered a large group of French Huguenots because of religious and political differences. A fort was built near the place where the slaughter occurred to protect the Mantanzas Inlet at the southern end of Anastasia Island. This inlet was considered the "back door" of St. Augustine, with the Castillo de San Marcos guarding the front.

The Mantanzas River, sometimes called the Mantanzas Bay, is the body of water that separates the St. Augustine mainland from Anastasia Island. It is also home to an important marshy habitat for many animals. The grasses in the marsh serve as a food source and shelter for a variety of animals. Some species prefer to eat the animals that feed on the grasses. Take a minute to visit St. Augustine's marshes and you are sure to see some of the many animals that feed, live, or even breed in the marsh there. Some of the animals to watch for include manatees, alligators, otters, raccoons, bobcats, fiddler crabs, and a variety of other insects, birds, and fish.

N is for the nests turtles dig on summer nights
on St. Augustine's beaches and fill with spheres of white.
Mother turtle was born on this same beach, many years ago.
Her children will lay their own eggs here in twenty years or so.

The loggerhead and green turtle are the two species of turtles known to lay their eggs on the beaches near St. Augustine. Between May and October these turtles crawl out of the Atlantic Ocean and onto the beach. Once there, they dig a hole in the sand and lay around 115 eggs. Then they bury their eggs in the sand and return to the ocean. About 60 days later, the baby turtles hatch from the eggs and emerge from the sand. They quickly scamper back to the ocean where they spend the rest of their lives. About 20 years later when the baby turtles are ready to lay their own eggs, they'll return to the same beach they were born on to build their nests.

Unfortunately, many of the baby turtles do not survive to build their own nests. Many turtle nests are destroyed by raccoons, dogs running loose on the beach, or people. Lights from houses along the beach confuse the baby turtles that are looking for the moon to guide them to the ocean. For the baby turtles that do make it to the sea, there are many predators waiting for them. Some local residents help the baby turtles survive by joining a sea turtle watch group that finds the nests along the beach and marks them for protection.

O is for Osceola, the Seminole war chief
who was captured in St. Augustine but only by deceit.
Osceola had fought in the Seminole Wars against the USA.
He agreed to meet to sign a truce but was captured and locked away.

Osceola was a war chief of the Seminole Indian tribe during the Second Seminole War that took place in Florida in the first half of the 1800s. The United States was attempting to remove the Seminoles from land they had lived on for many years. Osceola helped lead the Seminoles against the United States.

In 1837, Osceola agreed to meet General Thomas Jesup near St. Augustine in order to negotiate a truce. However, when Osceola arrived, Jesup and his men captured him instead of trying to make peace. Osceola was locked in the Castillo de San Marcos. He was soon moved to another fort in South Carolina where he died.

P is for Ponce de Leon, the Spaniard
who loved to explore,
and who was the first European to set foot
on the sandy St. Augustine shore.
He explored the whole peninsula and
claimed the land for Spain.
He also discovered the Gulf Stream waters
and gave the state its name.

Juan Ponce de Leon's adventures to the New World began in 1493 when he joined Christopher Columbus on his second voyage there. He would make more journeys to the Caribbean and was eventually named provincial governor of the island that would become Puerto Rico. During this time, rumors ran wild that there were undiscovered lands northwest of Puerto Rico called the Islands of Bimini. Ponce de Leon was given a royal contract to search for these in 1512. On April 2, 1513, Ponce de Leon saw a new land that he thought was an island. He named it La Florida after the flowers he saw there and in honor of the Easter season (the Spanish called Easter Pascua Florida which meant Festival of Flowers).

What he had discovered, of course, was the Florida peninsula. Ponce de Leon and his men soon landed around the area that is now St. Augustine. The men didn't stay long though as they continued to explore the Florida coast. They later discovered the Florida Keys and the Gulf Stream which would allow Spanish ships quick passage back to Spain.

Q is for quadricentennial, a celebration of 400 years
since Pedro Menendez of Spain established a mission here.
To celebrate this 400th anniversary of the events of 1565
a large steel cross was constructed, that reaches 208 feet high.

In 1565 King Philip II of Spain put Pedro Menendez in charge of 30 ships carrying 2,650 men with orders to conquer the Florida peninsula. By the time land was spotted on August 28th, only about 600 of those men had survived the trip across the ocean. Menendez continued to explore the coast by ship before finally landing on the area that would become St. Augustine on September 8th. A small fort and settlement were made at the landing site and the Spanish flag was raised.

To mark the 400th anniversary, or quadricentennial, of this event, a celebration was held in 1965. A 208-foot-tall stainless steel cross was erected at the site and named the Beacon of Faith. An outdoor theater, called an amphitheatre, was also constructed that was home to a play called *Cross and Sword*. The play was about St. Augustine's beginnings and ran for more than 30 years.

Mission of Nombre De Dios

SHRINE OF OUR LADY OF LA LECHE

R is for the roar of the lion, the mascot of Flagler College
where students come from all around to increase their worldly knowledge.
The school is housed in the hotel that Flagler built many years past.
Hotel rooms were converted so professors could teach their class.

Flagler College is a small liberal arts college. It was founded as a woman's college in 1968 but began accepting men in 1971. Today it hosts around 3,000 students. The college was established by Lawrence Lewis, Jr., who was one of Henry Flagler's heirs. The Ponce de Leon Hotel was given to the college and is still the main building on campus today. Various rooms of the hotel were converted to offices and classrooms. Other buildings have been added to the campus over time. Some of those buildings are modern while others are historically significant. The school's most popular majors are in the fields of business, communications, and education. The college's mascot is the lion, but their nickname is the Saints..

S is for Seloy, the Indian village that thrived
in the area that is now St. Augustine before the Spanish arrived.
These Indians were Timucuans who wore unusually tall hairdos.
They also covered their bodies in elaborate tattoos.

Before the Europeans came to the New World and settled Florida, there was an Indian village called Seloy where St. Augustine is now. It was very near Seloy that Pedro Menendez built his mission when he first came to the area. In fact, the chief of Seloy agreed to give him the land. The Indians that lived at Seloy were from the Timucuan tribe, and they had lived in the area for thousands of years. They liked to cover their bodies with large tattoos using ink from plants found in the area. They also wore their hair pulled up high on their heads. The Timucuans made good use of the resources available to them. They grew many crops including corn, beans, pumpkins, and squash. They also hunted and ate the animals that lived around them.

The Timucuans' favorite meal might have been oysters, though. The Indians walked through the marsh and gathered the oysters wherever they could find them. Usually, they would eat the oysters as soon as they found them and then would throw their shells on the ground. Throwing oyster shells on the ground for thousands of years made some big piles of shells which can still be seen today. They are called middens and sometimes contain other Timucuan pottery and arrow heads.

T is for the tourists and the tourism industry.

St. Augustine is great for vacations because there's lots to do and see.
These tourists eat at restaurants and stay in the great hotels.
The money that they spend creates many jobs as well.

The tourism industry is very important to St. Augustine. While the town has had its share of visitors all along, it became a popular tourist destination when Henry Flagler began building his hotels and trains in the Ancient City. After Flagler's hotels were complete, St. Augustine's popularity took off. The town was known as the "Newport of the South," and many tourists from the North came to enjoy the warm climate. Attractions like Marineland, The Alligator Farm, and The Fountain of Youth soon sprang up and kept tourists visiting the town after the railroad's popularity fell.

Today tourists continue to visit St. Augustine for the attractions, weather, and the beaches. They need places to sleep and eat which means hotels and restaurants do quite well. Tourists also like to shop and many gift stores cater to them. The restaurants, hotels, and shops provide lots of jobs and are very important to the St. Augustine economy.

U is for the German U-boats from the Second World War
waiting to attack the ships and towns along the Atlantic's shore.
Men were placed in the lighthouse to watch carefully from their post
for German submarines lurking off St. Augustine's coast.

During the 1940s, the United States was in a bitter war with Germany. This war included many other countries and is known as World War Two. The Germans had a powerful army and navy. The main threat Germans held in their navy was their fleet of *unterseeboots*, which means undersea boat in German. In English, we call most undersea boats submarines. However, we call the German submarines of the 1940s "U-boats."

German U-boats were spread out all over the world during World War Two. Some of them lurked right off the Atlantic coast, waiting to sink American ships or attack American towns. St. Augustine was no exception. Coast Guardsmen sat in the St. Augustine Lighthouse looking for German U-boats in the ocean. Other citizens of the town volunteered to do the same from area beaches.

V is for Victorian, an architectural design that still
marks many homes and businesses in neighborhoods like Lincolnville.
In the late 1800s this style was all the rage.
The collection at the Lightner Museum also reminds us of that age.

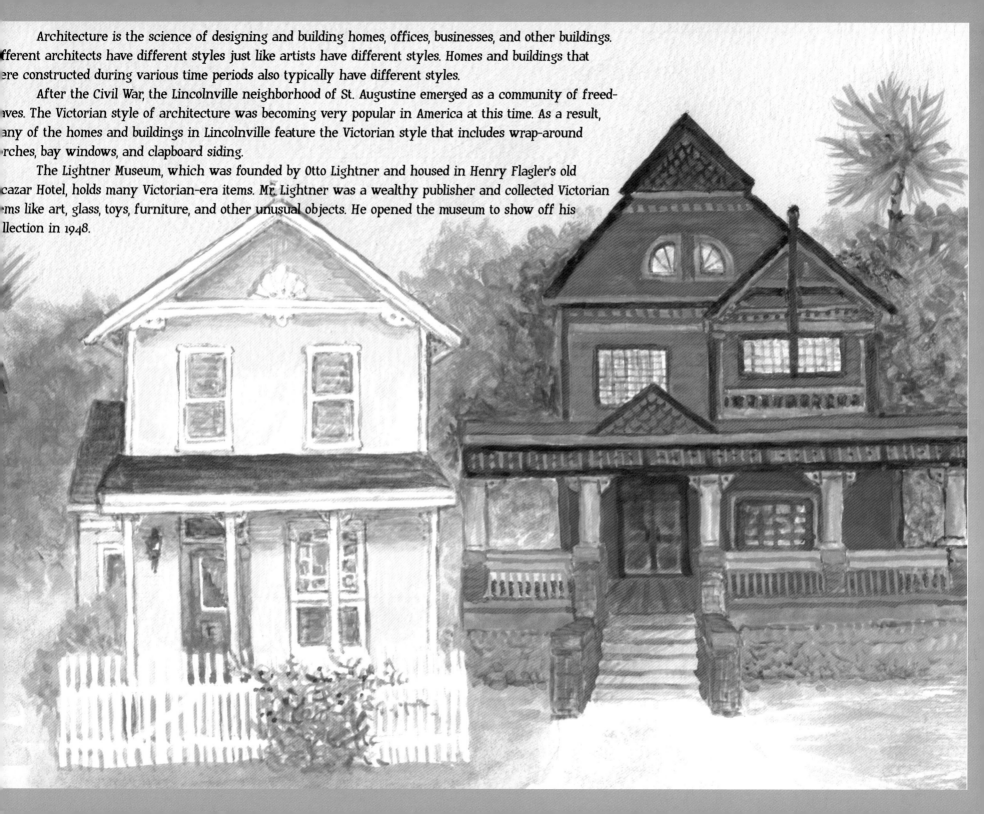

Architecture is the science of designing and building homes, offices, businesses, and other buildings. Different architects have different styles just like artists have different styles. Homes and buildings that were constructed during various time periods also typically have different styles.

After the Civil War, the Lincolnville neighborhood of St. Augustine emerged as a community of freed-slaves. The Victorian style of architecture was becoming very popular in America at this time. As a result, many of the homes and buildings in Lincolnville feature the Victorian style that includes wrap-around porches, bay windows, and clapboard siding.

The Lightner Museum, which was founded by Otto Lightner and housed in Henry Flagler's old Alcazar Hotel, holds many Victorian-era items. Mr. Lightner was a wealthy publisher and collected Victorian items like art, glass, toys, furniture, and other unusual objects. He opened the museum to show off his collection in 1948.

W is for the World Golf Hall of Fame
that honors the past of a favorite game.
The shops, restaurants, and theatre here add to the St. Augustine fun.
You can even head out to the greens and try to hit a hole-in-one.

The World Golf Hall of Fame was built in St. Augustine in 1998. It is part of the World Golf Village which is home to many shops and restaurants with golf-related themes. It is also home to an IMAX theatre. The World Golf Hall of Fame is supported by 26 golf organizations. It honors men and women golfers, young and old. This wasn't the first professional golf hall of fame, though. Several others existed before it, but over time these organizations merged together and they are now part of the World Golf Hall of Fame, which honors golf greats like Jack Nicklaus, Arnold Palmer, and Nancy Lopez.

There are, naturally, golf courses at the World Golf Village and several other courses around town. Many of these were designed by some of the best known golf course designers in the world. Scores of tourists come to St. Augustine just to enjoy these golf courses.

X comes from excavations, done all over town.
From Indian villages to Spanish missions, there's a lot of history underground.
These "digs" are a form of archaeology where researchers hope to find
relics and other artifacts that our ancestors left behind.

Excavation is a form of archaeology, which is the study of
ancient things. Our ancestors left many things behind like their tools,
parts of their homes, or bones from the animals they ate. Often, these
things were just our ancestors' garbage. Over time, Mother Nature
covered these things up. In an excavation, archaeologists work very
carefully to remove earth from areas thought to be the former homes
of ancient people or animals. As they work, they search for these
treasures our predecessors left us. They can use these things to learn
more about the life and times of those who came before us.
Since the archaeologists are essentially digging large holes
in the ground, excavations are often called "digs."

Many excavations have been done around
St. Augustine. The remains of the Indian village
of Seloy, for example, were found near the
Fountain of Youth Archaeological Park as
well as the remnants of the Spanish
Mission that was there. Other pieces
of St. Augustine's Spanish influence
have been found all over town, and
there are surely other historic
items that still lay hidden
underground.

Y is for the youthful fountain and the legend that was told
of rejuvenating waters that could keep one from growing old.
As Ponce de Leon was exploring Florida, he was searching for the Fountain of Youth.
Or so the story says; most question the legend's truth.

The legend of the Fountain of Youth has been told for centuries. The waters of the fountain could supposedly restore youth and vitality to older people. While the story has been told in different cultures, it is most closely tied to Juan Ponce de Leon. The legend says that the natives of Puerto Rico told him about the fountain's existence when he visited the island. Thus, Ponce de Leon headed out in search of it and discovered Florida along the way. Ponce de Leon's connection to the fountain was published in a book after his death and nothing in his own writings suggest he was looking for the fountain. That is why most people think the legend is just a story.

An area in St. Augustine is now designated as the Fountain of Youth Archaeological Park. This 15-acre park is home to a small fountain and is believed by some to be the site where Ponce de Leon first landed in Florida. The area was the previous home of the Indian village of Seloy. The park also hosts several archeological points of interest and several species of birds including peacocks.

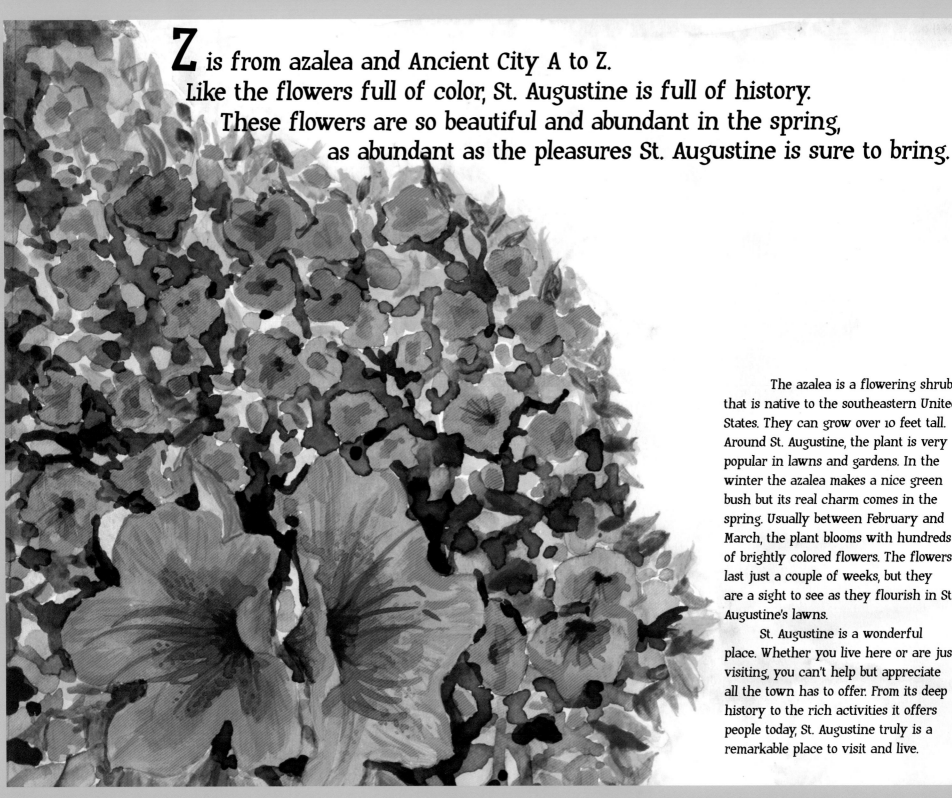

Z is from azalea and Ancient City A to Z.
Like the flowers full of color, St. Augustine is full of history.
These flowers are so beautiful and abundant in the spring,
as abundant as the pleasures St. Augustine is sure to bring.

The azalea is a flowering shrub that is native to the southeastern United States. They can grow over 10 feet tall. Around St. Augustine, the plant is very popular in lawns and gardens. In the winter the azalea makes a nice green bush but its real charm comes in the spring. Usually between February and March, the plant blooms with hundreds of brightly colored flowers. The flowers last just a couple of weeks, but they are a sight to see as they flourish in St. Augustine's lawns.

St. Augustine is a wonderful place. Whether you live here or are just visiting, you can't help but appreciate all the town has to offer. From its deep history to the rich activities it offers people today, St. Augustine truly is a remarkable place to visit and live.